inspire
creative
writing

Stephen May

Hodder Education
338 Euston Road, London NW1 3BH.

Hodder Education is an Hachette UK company

First published in UK 2011 by Hodder Education.

Copyright © 2011 Stephen May

British Library Cataloguing in Publication Data: a catalogue record for this title
is available from the British Library.

10 9 8 7 6 5 4 3 2 1

www.hoddereducation.co.uk

Typeset by MPS Limited, a Macmillan Company.
Printed in Great Britain by CPI Cox & Wyman, Reading.

Contents

Acknowledgements

Warm thanks and appreciation to Camilla Hornby, Ilona Jones, Caron May, Carol and Charles Ockleford, Victoria Roddam and all the writers who have helped contribute to this project.

1

why write?

Unlike learning to master a musical instrument, writing does not demand hours and hours of repetitive practice every day. Nor, like many sports or hobbies, does it demand expensive equipment. And neither is it like learning a language: you don't need to go abroad, or find someone else to practise with.

All you need is a pen, some paper and a place to write. And it doesn't need to a particularly private place. You can write on the tube, on the bus, in a café, during breaks or stolen moments at work. You can write in bed.

You don't need to be in perfect health or even physically fit. You don't have to have a degree, or even a GCSE. You don't have to be young. You don't have to be good-looking. You don't have to be a certain social class. Writing is completely democratic.

You just need something to say.

Writing is easy

More or less every adult in this country can write. Despite what we read and hear, teachers are not doing so bad a job that many pupils leave school illiterate. Most of us can fashion a sentence, however clumsily. In addition, many people who would never consider themselves to be writers can use words very well. Think of the people you know at work, or among your friends and family, who are natural storytellers – people who can hold a group enthralled with a vivid account of something that happened to them, or who can get a room to explode in laughter with a quick one-liner. There is every likelihood that you know many people who are famed among their peers for their skill with words, and not one of them would consider themselves to be a writer. There are people whose emails or texts are a joy to read because they have a special colour with which they use language, even if it is dealing with something really quite dull. The famous Czech writer Franz Kafka had a day-job as an insurance clerk but by all accounts, his reports and minutes were eagerly awaited by his colleagues because of their dry humour and elegant phrasing.

Exercise 1

Write down in one sentence (no more than 30 words) why it is that you want to write.

Writing is natural

The philosopher Socrates said 'The unexamined life is not worth living' and *his* words, as transcribed by Plato, have survived for several thousand years, so he knew what he was talking about. We live busy lives at a frantic pace. There often doesn't seem time just to 'stand and stare' as the poet W. H. Davies put it.

We spend so much of our time firefighting – reacting to events – that we leave ourselves little time to investigate the causes of all the small blazes in our lives. Why do we do the things we do? Why do we often feel hurt, neglected or sad? How can we be better parents, children, companions or lovers? How can we make sense of a world that contains 6 billion people? What is the point of it all?

For some people their natural mode of self-expression will be one of the other arts. They will form a band, or join a choir. They might take photographs or paint. Others will want to act or make films or create conceptual art. Still others will find that the extraordinary advances in digital technology will lead them down pathways to self-expression that didn't even exist ten years ago. But more and more of us, even in a digital world, want to use one of the oldest and simplest forms of self-expression. We want to tell stories. We want to tell our own stories or make up new ones. We want to transform our own existence into words that will delight, entertain, amuse or even horrify others.

Creative writing is good for you

Writing is a good way to reduce stress and relieve depression. Simply writing troubles down makes them seem more manageable. Reliving past traumas on the page can reduce their power to haunt. Writing is a way of taking control over your life. Therapy might not be your primary motivation for becoming a writer, but writing is certainly an effective way of keeping anxiety at bay. In fact, I can say that if you write regularly you will look and feel better without even needing to get up from your chair! It is that powerful a magic.

Creative writing is sociable

This might seem an odd thing to say: the usual image of a writer is someone who is solitary, a hermit. And it is true that in order to write successfully you need to have the ability and the discipline to shut yourself off in a room on your own. But writers also form a community and as we begin to take our work more seriously, the more important that community will be to us.

Playwrights for example, work closely with the directors and actors. But even for poets and novelists the need for peer support can be incredibly important. As you become more confident with your writing you will probably want to join a local group of fellow writers. You will want to find supportive but candid friends who can act as first readers and trusted guides. You will also find personal benefits in providing this service for other people. You might want to attend intensive residential courses like those run by the Arvon Foundation. You might even end up deciding to undertake an MA in Creative Writing. But whatever paths writing leads you down you are bound to end up meeting like-minded people who are stimulating – sometimes infuriating – to be around.

Exercise 2

Using the library, the internet or the local press, find out if there are any writing groups nearby. Get the contact numbers and call them to see how they work and whether they would be suitable for you to join.

Creative writing is cheap and accessible

If you want to be a top sports pro it is unlikely that you are going to be able to get one-to-one tuition from the very best players and coaches. But in the field of creative writing your perfect mentors are always around, always available. If you use your public library then your favourite authors are there, they are free, and they are present for as long as you need them. There is absolutely nothing to stop you spending weeks locked up alone with Tolstoy, or with Philip Roth, Sharon Olds, Sylvia Plath, Jackie Collins or Woody Allen.

Exercise 3

Make a short list of the writers whose works you have found most inspiring. Now make sure that you fit in a trip to the public library when you next go shopping and take out some of their work. Reacquaint yourself with your heroes.

Exercise 4

This is about trying to find some new heroes. Ask around among your friends, family and work colleagues for examples of writing that they have found particularly impressive. When you return your heroes to the library, make sure you replace them with some writing that has been recommended to you. Reading, more than anything else, is what will help you to improve as a writer. Reading good work carefully is the fastest way to see visible developments in your own writing life. And it helps to have an open mind and a willingness to experiment in your reading tastes too. Try not to be too dismissive of work you see being championed in the press or on television. On the other hand, reading something and then thinking, 'I could do better than that' is a perfectly legitimate response. It can be very inspiring to find some writer who has legions of admirers but who you think is not actually such hot stuff. That's fine. I'd keep it to yourself for a little while, however!

Creative writing is a family affair

Writing creatively is a good way to get and stay close to your family. Older family members may well have interesting stories and family secrets that can act as springboards for your own work. Your children and other younger relatives may want to know about the stories that you can tell. Very young children, of course, love stories, whether real or imagined, and are a very good and truthful audience.

Exercise 5

Ask someone in your extended family for a story that they haven't told you before. They don't have to be convinced that it is entirely true, it could be some kind of family legend from the distant past. Take notes and put them in a drawer to be worked on later.

Finding time to write

Everyone has time to write. It might be that something else will have to go (a favourite television show, an hour's sleep), but you'll find the time to write if you want to badly enough. Suzanne Berne, the Orange prize-winning author of *A Crime in the Neighborhood*, wrote her first book having been determined to set aside at least five minutes a day in which to write. If she achieved at least her daily five minutes then she gave herself a little tick on her calendar. 'After a little while,' she says, 'I became obsessed with giving myself a tick every day. And if you can somehow manage a page a day, that's a novel in a year.'

The double Carnegie medal-winning children's author Berlie Doherty put a log on the fire after her children went to bed and wrote until the log burnt out. Serious writers, those who make a success of it, will make time.

However much or little you write, regularity is the most important thing. Suzanne Berne's five minutes a day will achieve better results than a four-hour stretch every now and again.

The second-best time

There's a saying: 'The best time to plant a tree is 20 years ago. The second-best time is now.' Of course you should really have got down to writing before this. But writing is one of those things that you can begin at any age. It doesn't require physical fitness, youth or even good health.

You have got to have lived a bit, and looked and listened a lot, before you have enough to say. Everything that has happened to you up to now is your material. The older you are the more material you have to draw on. You are in a better position than someone just out of college. Wordsworth described writing as 'experience recollected in tranquillity'. And so the more experience you have the better. You just need to make sure that you can find those moments of tranquillity!

A word about technology

You don't need a laptop to be a writer. And having one doesn't make you a writer either. A light, simple-to-use laptop might be very useful, but it is by no means essential. The great Californian crime writer Peter Plate once found himself facing students upset that a temporary power failure meant that the computers weren't working in the building where he was conducting a writing class. His calm response made a powerful impression on me. He said, 'Don't confuse convenience with utility'. And with that he sent everyone off to write with a pencil.

Now, I'm not so much of a Luddite as to suggest that new writers should get rid of their PCs – for one thing the internet can be an important market for a writer as well as a valuable research tool – but we should all be aware that just because our work looks professionally solid in its beautiful font, it doesn't mean that the writing itself is any good. The comfort that modern technology brings means that we have to be strict with ourselves.

The next chapter explores how to find ideas and inspiration that will unlock your authentic voice and so begin to create the writing that is distinctively yours, but before that here is a simple exercise that helps you realize just how subtle great writing can be.

Exercise 6

Go to a book you love. Open it at random and copy out a paragraph. That's it. (Poets will want to copy out a poem.) Repeat this process two or three times with different books. It will give you a physical sense of how that writing was built up. Teachers of other art forms, such as music or painting, are very keen on getting practitioners to copy before they move on to original modes of expression. For obvious reasons writers haven't intentionally copied other people's work since the invention of the printing press. But a small taste of it in this way can be quite helpful in bringing you close to the rhythm and pulse of your favourite writers. It's a way of giving you a physical sense of how they go about building effective passages of writing.

2

ideas and inspirations

This chapter is about generating ideas. Ideas are tricky little creatures. There are always millions around. More than enough for all the writers that have ever been. One sort are free-range, scuttling through your head at all sorts of odd times. These can be fleeting, shy, even ghostly animals that are hard to catch. For this reason if you take just one thing from this whole book, it's to always carry a notebook.

If you can corral your ideas into a book, then you've a chance of developing them, training them, feeding them up so that you can see which have the capacity to really go places, and which were actually fairly feeble and can be set free again. And your notebook needn't be a fancy one, a school exercise book will do. It needn't be an actual book even: I've seen authors use phones to record their thoughts.

Inspiration does exist... but it has to find you working.

Pablo Picasso

Generating your own ideas

Some useful ideas may hurtle out of the sky, or scurry through your mind as if from nowhere. Others you may have to nurture from scratch. Either way, the blank page is always a tyrant to any writer, which is why so many start the day with automatic or free writing. Anything to stop the oppression of all that white space.

Exercise 7

Try your hand at free writing. Set an alarm clock, cell phone or kitchen timer to go off after five minutes and just keep writing for the whole of that time. Don't allow your conscious mind to interfere, just keep writing. Keep your pen moving for the whole period. At least one useful nugget will emerge that might be worked on later. More than this, however, the act of writing, under pressure but without an editor or critic in your head, will help loosen you up for the challenges of your current writing project.

Many, many writers are fervent believers in the idea of morning pages: of getting up and writing first thing, before you have had a coffee, showered or washed your face. This, they believe, is when you are most in touch with your subconscious self and able to tap into the rich seams of material that gets buried during the working day.

Many writers conscientiously keep dream diaries as repositories of the strange wisdom that comes to us all in the night, and which we can draw on later when creating our polished work.

Using what only you know

There are exercises that can help force ideas to the surface the way that beaters are employed to force game birds into the sky for the hunters to bag.

Exercise 8

Writing what you know is probably the single most common piece of advice handed out to a new writer. And it clearly makes sense, as this exercise shows.

1 Draw up a list of all the jobs you have had.
2 Now write down all the places you have been to in the last five years.
3 Write down all the places you have ever lived.
4 Add to this list all the people whom you have worked with.
5 Write down your hobbies and interests.
6 Write down the names, jobs or interests of all the people you know best.

You should by now have pages and pages of possible material. Suddenly there in front of you are tremendous possibilities for exciting writing that no one else can produce. No one else has quite this collection of characters, settings, stories or experiences. This exercise is a great one for making concrete the sheer wealth of material you have at your fingertips.

Here is a simple exercise that I first saw used in a workshop by the poets Colette Bryce and Matthew Hollis and it's great for making you think about your parents in a new light.

Exercise 9

Try to imagine your parents together before you were born. Try and place them in a specific situation, doing something together. Are they on honeymoon? On holiday? Or visiting friends? Are they quietly sitting side-by-side in the evening or are they arguing passionately, fiercely about something? Is there harmony in this situation or conflict? Are they in a town or a house you know well, or somewhere where you have never been? Do they have brothers or sisters on the scene or are they alone? Or are they with their parents perhaps?

See if you can write just 100 or 200 words on this.

Including what you don't know

Here is an exercise that stresses the importance of making every word count. It's great as an ice-breaker but it also builds on what has gone before and introduces one key new element. This time you are not only writing about what you know best – yourself – but you are also writing what you *don't* know. This is every bit as much of a writer's job as drawing on your own experience. Making stuff up is part of the job description.

Exercise 10

Your task is to write your autobiography in exactly 50 words. Not 49. Not 51. Exactly 50. And it must also contain one lie. As an example, here is one that I did...

> *Stephen May was a sickly child. Born in Norfolk, schooled in Bedford but with Scottish parents. He has been a barman, a journalist, a warehouseman, a teacher and a model. He was also thrown out of his teenage punk band after being seen dancing to Abba records at a party.*

Naturally, I'm not going to tell you what my lie is...

Using magazines and newspapers

These can be great inspirations for your own writing. Usually the headline stories won't be the things that capture your imagination. It can be the smaller snippets that lead you to think 'What if...', which leads on to, 'Let's pretend...'. The poet Amanda Dalton kept an article for years about a woman who abandoned her house to live in the garden, building a kind of nest out there from leaves and twigs and bits of rubbish. Her fascination with this woman and the possible reasons for her leading this life grew at last into the sequence of poems called 'Room of Leaves' in her first collection (*How To Disappear* – published by Bloodaxe) and then into an acclaimed radio play. The initial story was just a few lines long but it planted itself in her imagination, growing to fruition over months and years.

Exercise 11

Look through today's newspapers. Is there a story there that intrigues you, that excites your curiosity? Something where you want to know more about the characters than the writer is telling you? Cut it out and save it to work on later. Or maybe paste it into your notebook.

The essential thing is to be receptive to all the ideas that are out there. For a writer everything is material to be processed, transformed, celebrated or examined. Be open to taking inspiration from anywhere, however unlikely a source. There are millions of stories, poems, plays, films and articles in circulation already, but none of them say what only you can say in the way that only you can say it.

Once you start to wander through the world – preferably with your notebook in your hand – looking at the world through writer's eyes, you will see that almost everything can be mined for material. Don't worry too much at this stage about being original. It's far, far better to be good.

3

the short story

In this chapter I'm going to give you what I consider to be the essential ingredients for a successful short story. In the preface to his book *The Modern Short Story*, H. E. Bates says that it is 'the most difficult and exacting of prose forms'. This is an accepted point of view and yet it is the form that beginners to writing are encouraged to attempt before going on to the long haul of the novel.

And there's sense in this. All writer's need to learn to write with economy, to draw a character in a few deft strokes of the pen. All writers need to learn about how to structure a piece that takes the reader on a journey. And there's nothing like finishing a piece, however short, to encourage a writer to move on and develop further.

Some common mistakes

The most common mistake is to try to be too dramatic. Novice writers often try and make an impression by shock. It's a tactic best avoided. Unless a new writer is very skilled it will be hard to persuade a reader to be led down the darkest alleyways.

Another mistake is to offer up as a story the unaltered anecdote. If you have a job where you mix a lot with people you are bound to have a fund of funny stories. But what is funny at a party doesn't always work on the page. The same is true of those writers who simply give us their unvarnished personal experiences, however shocking or powerful. This is not to decry the value of writing these down. Often they can be the springboard for producing honed and developed pieces. And making sense of our own lives is at least part of the point of all writing.

There needs to be craft, care and thought in a written story. Readers are far more acute and unforgiving than an audience at a social gathering.

The ingredients

To produce an interesting short story you will need an original idea, believable characters, a convincing background, a good opening, conflict, suspense, a sense of shape and a satisfying ending.

It's obvious, isn't it? And yet these ingredients are by no means always easy to find. And you cannot do without one of these, or find a simple, more accessible substitute.

Finding short story ideas

In Chapter 2 we talked about how ideas need to be hunted down and corralled. The germ of a short story could also come from an overheard conversation or a fragment of something that was on television or radio. Or you could try one of these exercises in order to generate ideas. They are both good ways of involving other people in your writing. The more involved they feel the more supportive they are likely to be and your life as a writer will be much easier if your partner, friends and family feel included in your efforts.

Exercise 12

You will need some close friends or members of your writing group to help you. Everyone should write down a secret which they fold up and place in a hat, a bag or a box. Draw out a secret and use it as a springboard for a story. If you are doing this in a writing group you should all meet again and swap the stories you developed from each other's secrets.

Exercise 13

Use photographs. Whatever kind of writer you are it's a good idea to get into the habit of collecting photographs and postcards. Anything that grabs your eye should be snapped up and placed safe in a box somewhere. On a day when the ideas just don't seem to want to come, you can go to the box and pick out a photo at random. It's probably best to choose one that you collected such a long time ago that you had forgotten you'd got it.

Spend ten minutes free writing about the photograph. Now use the photo – or a detail from it – as a starting point for your story.

Finding believable characters

The most important task for the short story writer is to choose the right central character. Unlike a novel, a short story usually revolves around one person whose problem becomes increasingly interesting. The reader needs to know and care about this person and so it is probably helpful to restrict yourself to a single viewpoint throughout the story. In other words, see everything through one character's eyes. Make sure in choosing your character that *you* sympathize with their plight. If you don't, then it is unlikely that any of your readers will care either. At this stage in your writing career it might be a good idea to write using the first person. Your readers are more likely to identify more easily with an 'I' character.

Dialogue is essential in a short story. People reveal themselves by the things they say and readers will feel that they know your characters far better if they can hear their unique voices.

Short stories are where eccentrics can often find a suitable fictional home. Here is an exercise that has often been used very effectively for finding characters and their voices.

Exercise 14

Take yourself off into your nearest town or village. Spend some time really looking at your fellow citizens. Find someone who is as different from yourself as you can. Someone much older, say. Or much younger. And follow them. Keep a discreet distance but stay close enough to be able to watch how they move. If they are with companions, try and overhear what they say. You could even begin this exercise in a café, overhearing what your fellow customers are talking about and then following a selected target as he or she leaves the premises. Try and gather as much information about your target's life as you can and then, safely back at home, make some detailed notes. This should give you enough material on which to base a central character.

A convincing background

Your characters should move in a realistic setting, though you don't want to spend a lot of time evoking it. Your job as a short story writer is to take your readers into the imaginary world and make them believe in it immediately.

It is probably a good idea to choose the kind of setting that you know well. And think about all the senses. Smells and sounds are as important as the way things look. And taste and touch can be as evocative too.

A good opening

A good short story needs to get going quickly. Your main character needs to make an appearance straightaway. You must arouse your reader's curiosity within the first page. Ideally, the first paragraph should be arresting. If the story doesn't really get going until page three, then throw away pages one and two. It might be that you as a writer need the first two pages, but the reader doesn't.

Conflict

'Happiness writes white' they say. In other words, contentment rarely makes for powerful stories. In a piece of short fiction you will need to ensure that your characters face problems from the start. They should be beset with difficulties and enemies and conflict.

Here is an exercise from the American Orange prize-winner Suzanne Berne and it's designed to allow you to develop conflict without succumbing to the temptation to become overblown.

Exercise 15

Describe a ritual that you have. Everyone has rituals, things they do to control their environment. It might be the way that you make tea, or a routine you have when going to work. Now imagine a break in that routine. What happens if the kettle doesn't work? Or a bus breaks down? Imagine the chain of events that might develop from there. Then imagine that you meet the person who has caused this disruption in your day. What might happen then? It's a good exercise for making it clear how small events can produce big emotional conflict.

Shape

Put simply this means that your story should have a beginning, a middle and an end. The beginning sets the scene, introduces the characters and poses the problem. The middle develops the action and explores the world of the story; and the end resolves the dilemmas of the central characters, for better or worse. Your task is to make sure that everything is relevant. Make sure that everything that might be irrelevant to the development of the story is jettisoned. Be hard on yourself and on your story.

Suspense

Your story should be plausible but never predictable. Having hooked your readers with a powerful or beguiling opening, you need to prevent them wriggling off. Avoid the temptation to depart from your main storyline or to get sucked into giving away too much back story about your characters. You might need to know where they went to school or how they met their first boyfriend but, unless it's absolutely essential to the story, your reader probably doesn't. It's about building tension: making the reader worry about what will happen next.

A good way to sketch out a plot is to keep building on that first dramatic scene. Each scene should suggest another. A lot of writers plan their plots before they write a word. And it's probably sensible. You should also give your characters choices as the story progresses. Different roads to take. Sometimes these should be the wrong roads. Your reader should want to scream at your characters, or to shake them. We should fall in love with some, and be irritated by others, but feel at least a little sympathy for all of them.

A satisfying ending

This doesn't need to be a happy one. Nor does it have to be one that ties up all the characters' relationships. It is perfectly possible to have a well-written, satisfying ending that leaves the possibilities open. With all stories it is important that you leave the reader some of the work to do. As the story progresses you will want to wrong-foot them and surprise them. But resist the temptation at the end to tell them everything that happens to the characters. Leave them to reflect and to wonder about the characters' futures. You don't necessarily have to have a dramatic twist either. That can look contrived. Unless it is very skilfully done it will just irritate a reader. While your story should end with some sort of emotional release for the reader, try to avoid doing this with a death. If you kill off your viewpoint character, then the reader will be disconcerted by wondering who is telling the story. And if you kill off the hero, or a character that the reader has come to like or to identify with, then you cause a little death in the heart of the reader too. As a general rule, when deaths occur in short stories they should happen at the beginning rather than the end.

Exercise 16

Choose a theme and central character for a short story. Make notes for a beginning, a middle and an end and write the first 500 words. You should by now have some substantial material from previous exercises.

Where to send your story

In the first place you should send your completed short story to a drawer. Print it off and leave it to sit and simmer for several weeks. While your story is lying apparently dormant in that drawer it will actually be cooking somewhere in your subconscious. When you do return to it, you will be amazed by how many flaws you find. Don't be downhearted by this. It's a necessary part of the process. Read your story through carefully, making notes in the margin. *Always* edit from a hard copy. Don't try and edit on-screen. You'll miss things. The experience of reading on-screen is very different from reading a printed page and it makes sense to come to your work in the same way that your reader will.

Once you've edited and revised and – probably – completely redrafted, send it back to the drawer to simmer some more. Then take it out and go through the editing, revising and redrafting process all over again. You might want to do this a few times.

When you are finally happy with your story you can start finding outlets for it. Don't feel nervous about this. You've worked hard on your story. It is very possible, likely even, that the first few stories you send out will attract rejections, but remember that we are choosing to see these as scars and battle honours, necessary bruises on the way to ultimate success.

poetry

Of all forms of writing, poetry is perhaps the most natural, but also the one most hedged around with rules. Everyone writes a kind of poetry at some time in their lives. At school it is almost the first thing we are encouraged to do. Almost as soon as the teacher has got us writing our names, then she's setting us the task of writing poems about 'Spring' or 'Christmas' or 'My Mum'.

As kids we set to with a will, spinning words into shapes that sound good. Children love rhyme and rhythm, wordplay and startling imagery. All the things that make writing memorable. And they can do it almost instinctively. It is for this reason that some writing by very young children can be so charming and so powerful. It is the childish spirit of mischief and play that we should be aiming for in all our writing, but perhaps especially in poetry.

Free verse

Most traditional verse forms have strict rules designed to force a poet to be creative rather than to go for the obvious. If you are forced to go for a word with a certain number of syllables then you are often driven away from your comfort zone and your usual vocabulary and into a more interesting place.

The great American poet Robert Frost said that 'writing free verse is like playing tennis with the net down'. By which he meant that it was without challenge or skill. Nevertheless it has become the dominant form of contemporary poetry, with the poet's theme being developed in a conversational style.

Here is an exercise from the award-winning poet Jean Sprackland. It's a good way of returning us to that sense of playing with words which we had as children, while at the same time getting us used to the idea that if it is any good, free verse is usually not as free as all that. There are usually constraints on the poet, even if they are self-imposed.

Exercise 17

Write the word 'autumn' on a blank piece of paper. Underneath list all the words that come to mind when you think of autumn. Spend a good five minutes doing this.

Now produce a poem that does not include any of the words in your list.

Writing poetry for yourself

No one writes poetry to become rich or famous. Probably the majority of poets don't even write for publication. Most poets write to make sense of the world, or to celebrate people, places, events or emotions that are particularly important to them. It's a powerful, almost primeval, impulse and its importance can be judged by the fact that at the most important of human moments – birth, love, death – people always reach for poetry. At heightened moments, heightened language is called for.

Here is a short poem that records one of these important rites of passage, which could be a trigger for your own personal memories and could spur you into writing the poem that only you can write. This is one of mine about the difficult birth of my youngest child.

'Surprise Party' by Stephen May

You weren't born so much as choked on:
coughed up and purple-black, translucent.
A half-sucked sweet. Plainly not ready for us,
the way that we were ready for you.
You were unmoved by the fanfare of bleeps,
the symphony of curses
from the handsome Slovak nurse.
The collision of panic and jargon
so familiar from Saturday night television.
You slept through it all while
I rehearsed funerals and teary phone calls and
cancelled everything.
When you deigned to cry
it was half-hearted, fitful,
as resentful as a schoolboy kept behind without cause. You were
unimpressed by all the sudden laughter
and high-fiving,
irritated by the giggles that fizzed into the ward
like Cava.

Exercise 18

You could try writing a poem about somewhere that has a personal significance to you. Try writing in the present tense as though it is all happening right now.

A word about rhyme

When most people think about poetry they think about rhyme. In particular they think about rhyming couplets or other simple end-rhymes, but the world of contemporary poetry is not keen on end-rhymes. Rhyme is still a weapon in the poet's armoury but it is to be used sparingly and in surprising ways. You are much more likely to find modern poets using rhyme within their lines, or breaking up their lines so that the rhyme is not immediately obvious. There is a good reason for this. It is hard to create end-rhymes that are fresh and original or that don't seem contrived. They can also unbalance a poem so that the ending of each line assumes exaggerated importance.

Reading poetry

It is said, and only half-jokingly, that there are far more poets than there are readers of poetry these days. It is true that poetry has fallen away from its position as the foremost of the written art forms. Since the advent of recorded music many people turn to song lyrics to find memorable words that express their emotions at important times in their lives. Pop music has replaced many of the functions of poetry. Nevertheless there is a thriving poetry scene in the UK, nurtured by bodies like the Poetry Society (see 'Taking it further'), and there are many more poetry readings than there ever used to be. As with all writing, it is only by reading widely and deeply in our chosen forms that we really improve. Unfortunately most bookshops only stock books by a few well-known poets and not many of them either. Libraries are better. And there are, of course, a wide range of magazines catering for all types of poetry.

Poetry readings

Listening to poets read can give us a completely new slant on their work. Often what has seemed difficult or obscure can become suddenly clear when we hear a poet's personal emphasis and stress. Reading out loud is also a great way to get a sense of whether your own poetry is working. Even if there is no one else listening there is something about hearing your work that makes you become suddenly alive to mistakes, clunky phrases, poor word choices and faulty rhythms. And the act of reading aloud seems to suggest replacements almost immediately.

Exercise 19

Take one of the poems you have written in previous exercises and read it aloud. Now make any changes you think are necessary. There will almost certainly be some and your work will almost certainly improve.

Exercise 20

A great way of generating new work is to find an object from your own home and write from its point of view. Think carefully about the function of your object and what it might have seen in its life. What might the future hold for it?

(This is an idea that is taken to a beautiful extreme in the novel *The Collector Collector* by Tibor Fischer which is narrated entirely by a Sumerian vase.)

When is a poem finished?

Somebody once said that poems 'aren't finished, they're abandoned'. And it's true that you could tinker with your work for months or years without it ever seeming quite perfect. I do suggest that when you think you have got an acceptable draft just put it away in a drawer for at least a few days. It is amazing just how many changes will suggest themselves to you when you revisit the piece later. Some poems will need to go through many drafts, while others will come together quite rapidly, but in the end only you will know whether you have done enough work on a poem, whether it is the very best that you can do. One Irish poet said to me that since poems were usually so much shorter than other forms of writing, we really owed it to all other writers to make sure that we worked and reworked them properly. This is the same poet who recalled his wife coming home and asking him how his day had gone. He had been pleased to be able to reply 'Good news! I got rid of three words today.'

On the other hand you don't want to linger too long over one piece of work; there are other poems to write. I once asked a famous poet how he managed to produce a collection every year when others seemed to leave an ice age between new books. His answer was, 'You should ask the others what they actually do with their time. Poems are only short, aren't they?'

Having a trusted candid reader, or members of a writing group, appraise your work can be very useful too. And the aforementioned Poetry Society will, for a modest fee, find established poets to produce critiques of your work.

Sending your work out

It should go without saying that you don't send your work out to a magazine you haven't even read. That just seems rude as well as pointless. It seems reasonable to become a subscriber to a few poetry magazines before you attempt to become a contributor to them. You should be familiar with the standard and style of the poems in a magazine before you send your own work. Don't be too disillusioned if your work seems very different from what they usually print. A fresh voice and an unusual approach to writing is your biggest asset. Editors are desperate to find good new writers that they can champion in their pages. The trouble is that they are often overwhelmed by hundreds, even thousands, of mediocre poems. No wonder that so many reputable magazines are starting to rely on recommendations from creative writing tutors, or other established poets, rather than trawling through the thousands of submissions that arrive on their desks daily.

Titles

A good, unusual title will usually ensure that an editor is intrigued enough to want to start reading and a good, arresting opening line is important too.

Practicalities

Send your target editor three or four poems, clearly typed, on one sheet of A4 paper and make sure you include your name and contact details; then wait. If you get a rejection letter, print the poems out again and send them off to the next magazine on your list.

If you want more information on how to write and publish poetry you should read *Write Poetry And Get It Published* by John Hartley-Williams and Matthew Sweeney.

5

creative non-fiction

Everyone tells real-life stories. Everyone comes home from even the simplest journey with an anecdote to tell. Something funny that happened to them or something they saw; a funny story told to them in a shop, or at work. We are a story-telling species. It is how we make sense of the world around us. How we get through the day.

For most people these stories are true. Real things that happened to real people in real places. Nevertheless everyone – often without realizing it – crafts their story. Shapes it in a way that makes it entertaining for the listener.

In this way everyone already has the basics for producing great non-fiction work instinctively. We all have the basic tools of transmuting our real experience into something compelling and I hope this chapter will help you develop this native ability.

What is creative non-fiction?

Creative non-fiction is becoming the most widely used term to cover memoir, biography, autobiography, travel writing and writing about historical events. All these kinds of writing have always been popular, but in recent years there has been an increase in demand for works in these genres. More than ever, audiences seem to crave 'authenticity' and 'real life'. The truth is that in order to work, non-fiction requires the same creative writing skills as those of fiction. It needs a solid structure, a compelling narrative voice and a clear connection of ideas. The 'truth' of your work will not necessarily be what engages your readers, it will be how well you present that truth.

Everyone has had important, dramatic, surprising things happen to them. Equally, every family history is filled with characters and dramas: little legends that demand telling. And the broad sweep of history too, features people who have been forgotten and neglected. People whose stories deserve retelling for new audiences. As the writer of these stories, whether your own or other people's, you will gradually become an expert in some area of life. Your area of expertise might be narrow, but nevertheless part of the appeal of becoming a writer of non-fiction is that you will be the authority on the stories you choose to tell.

Finding a subject

You perhaps already have an idea of the story you want to write. Perhaps you lived through an era or in a place others know little about. Or you just want to get your life down so that others in your family – children or grandchildren for example – understand what those times were like for you. Whatever the reason, you are probably excited by the idea of writing an autobiography.

It might be that there are family legends, tales passed down from your own parents and other older relatives, that you want to verify. There might be family characters whose lives seem worth exploring in more detail: a great-great uncle in the Royal Flying

Corps, a great-great aunt who was one of the original suffragettes. An ancestor who sailed to America in search of a better life or who was fleeing persecution or economic hardship. One person who attended a writing course at the Ted Hughes Arvon Centre wanted to tell the story of her great-grandmother, the original inspiration for the Alice in Wonderland stories. Another was inspired by finding his grandfather's wartime diaries that recorded his time as a Battle of Britain fighter pilot.

Other writers have ambitions that are slightly larger in scope. One who came to our writing centre wanted to tell the story of a World War I poet, a contemporary of Owen and Sassoon, who she felt had been unjustly ignored and about whom little seemed to be known. Other people are excited by the idea of travel and reflecting on their travels for themselves and for others.

This is a similar exercise to one that we did in Chapter 2, 'Ideas and inspirations', but it is a variation that might help show you the huge range of creative avenues open to you.

Exercise 21

Make a simple timeline of all the key moments in your life. You might begin with the most obvious: your birth.

You might end up with something like this:

Nicola Lawson

Born 1968 Watford
Began at Bash Street Infants, Watford September 1973
Moved to Nigeria for Dad's work August 1976
Returned to Watford July 1981, attended Enid Blyton High School
1984 Parents divorced, moved to Colchester
Met Danny Finch who became first boyfriend, beginning of
    Wild Years
June 1986 Dropped out of High School, left home
June 1988 Married Guy Peters
September 1989 First child Tamara born

September 1992 Divorced Guy Peters, attended access course at
   local college

October 1994 Enrolled at Greenwich University

June 1997 Graduated with first class honours in History

September 1997 Got job with Greenwich museum service

Attended evening classes in life-drawing where met Barry
   Rogerson

August 1999 Married Barry Rogerson

July 2001 Second child Elliot born

October 2003 Moved to Spain with Barry to run a bar

February 2005 Returned to England to look after mother who was
   seriously ill

February 2006 Sold bar, returned to England. At Luton airport
   daughter Tamara spotted by modelling agent and given contract
   one month later

February 2007 Picked up copy of Vogue with Tamara on the front
   cover. Decide to write book about year as mother of aspiring
   model.

   There's a lot here. And a lot that a reader could be interested
in. For example what exactly did Nicola do in her 'Wild Years'?
Why did her parents divorce? Why did her mother move from
Watford to Colchester after the divorce? What was life like
for a child spending a large part of her childhood in Nigeria?
What prompted Nicola to return to education? Why did her own
first marriage fail? What was Guy Peters like? What attracted
her to Barry Rogerson? Was he another student on the course?
The teacher? The model? What was life like in Spain as a bar owner
who was also trying to bring up a toddler? Why did she give up
work at the museum? Did she take her children with her when
she went back to look after her mum? Did her mother recover
and what was wrong with her anyway?

   And then there are the big questions posed by the facts
towards the end of Nicola's timeline: how did the modelling agent
approach her daughter? What was Nicola's reaction? Was she
suspicious? Delighted? And what were the stresses and strains
of being plunged into that world? How did their lives change?

How did Tamara cope with it all? What does Nicola feel about the modelling industry? Did she meet any interesting people? What does the future hold for the family now?

I have no doubt that your own timeline will be at least as interesting as this one and throw up as many questions and provide as many possibilities for future work.

What is clear though, is that if Nicola was telling her life story she probably wouldn't want to start right at the beginning. She herself made the decision that the most interesting thing for her to write about was the whole experience of becoming the mother of a young model.

She took an incident that happened late on in her timeline and took that as the subject of her first book. If she does it well that first book will be a mixture of memoir, a study of the fashion and modelling industries, and a biography of her daughter's short life. If she pulls it off it'll be a thought-provoking, entertaining read.

There were other avenues she could have gone down of course. Especially as I happen to know that her mother was the niece of the writer Georgina Basket, who produced popular detective novels in the 1940s. The same Georgina Basket who, family legend has it, was rumoured to have been a spy during World War II and dropped by parachute several times into occupied France in order to pass important messages to the Resistance.

She could also have written about the area of Spain where she and her second husband ran a bar. They lived in a small town, high in the Pyrenees, where Barry and Nicola and their children were the only English people and as such were objects of much curiosity. Fitting into the local community was often a challenge, particularly as they didn't speak the language and Barry never saw a reason to. Ultimately, however, the experience was rewarding despite all the difficult and comical moments along the way. Nicola, Barry and the children were sad to leave and one of the first things Tamara did when she became a successful model was to buy a cottage in the town.

She could also have written about her experience of getting divorced from Guy Peters, which was astonishingly amicable and, she feels, could easily be a template for others going through similarly awkward situations. Perhaps her next book will be a manual for a civilized divorce.

Or she could have written about the eminent Victorian explorer and philanthropist, Lady Freeborn of Whittlesea, whose letters she came across while studying for her dissertation at Greenwich University and whom she has always wanted to research. Any moderately active life will furnish similar possibilities.

Structure

Possibly the most important thing about any piece of writing is the opening and this is just as true for a piece of non-fiction writing as it is for a novel.

The most obvious structure for a memoir or a biography is that suggested by William Shakespeare at the beginning of *As You Like It*. You must know it. It's the 'Seven Ages of Man' sonnet that begins with 'All the world's a Stage/And all the men and women merely players'.

Shakespeare's Seven Ages begins with the infant 'mewling and puking in the nurse's arms' and moves on through the schoolboy, the lover, the soldier, the justice, and the lean and slippered pantaloon, before the seventh age of second childishness sans teeth, sans eyes, sans everything.

It is easy to imagine the memoirist or the biographer looking back from the point of view of the sixth or even seventh age, and beginning their recollections with all that mewling and puking before moving on steadily through the other ages. And it might easily be quite dull. In any case, is the birth of the subject even the start of his story? In the novel *Tristram Shandy* the narrator finds himself compelled to begin his life story from the moment of his conception, which means he has to describe the childhood of his parents and so on. The story hardly gets started. A modern reader wants to be pulled into the story straight away.

Create a timeline

Think of all the things you did yesterday. Make a list, starting with getting up and ending with going to bed. Now choose the most interesting thing that happened yesterday and write that down in as much detail as you can. I guarantee that at least one interesting thing happened yesterday. Try and capture it all. Describe the characters involved and where they were. Just stick to the who, the what, the where and the why. Keep it short.

Now complete this next exercise which focuses on one area of the timeline.

Go back to your timeline and pick a pivotal moment in your life. One incident that seemed to sum up where your life was going. It might be a row with a parent. A proposal of marriage. A stag or hen night. A job interview. The birth of a child. The arrival in a foreign country. It can be large or small, the important thing is that it is one vivid episode which has stayed with you for many years. Write it up as if you were telling it for the first time to an interested person who doesn't know you or anything about the people involved. Write it in the present tense as though the event is happening right now. Begin with the words 'I am...' and carry on from there. Again, keep it reasonably short, no more than 250 words. Try and set the scene; make the readers really feel like they are witnesses.

Example:

I am sitting in my father's chair. The leather armchair with the odd high back. We are waiting for him to come home, my mother and I. I have something important to say.

The point is that your memoir or biography needn't necessarily begin at the beginning and move forward from there. That is, of course, one way to do it, but it might be an idea to start with something that reveals something about the character, or something that foreshadows the kind of person your subject became.

Consider various viewpoints

Here is another exercise designed to help you think about the structure of a piece of creative non-fiction.

Exercise 24

Imagine that it is your funeral. Make notes about who will be there and who might be missing. Now imagine that a good friend is standing up to deliver the eulogy. What might they say about you? What stories might they tell, designed to show your character in all its eccentric humanity? (I already know that you are eccentric because you have decided to become a creative writer!) Crucially, what might they leave out in telling your story to the assembled congregation?

Being selective is a skill of all writing and it is especially true of non-fiction writing. What *not* to write is every bit as important as deciding what to put in and where. At a funeral each speaker has just a few minutes to deliver a monologue about the deceased, so your eulogy to yourself will need to be just a few pages long but has still to cover the most important facts of your life and to tell a few good stories too. It's not easy is it? But it's possibly the most useful exercise in structure there is and you may well find out something about yourself as well.

If you find the idea of writing your own funeral address too depressing you could try preparing a best man's speech for your own wedding, or a father's speech if you are a bride. The problems are still the same: what goes in, what stays out and what order do you place the events in?

Of course the exercise above assumes that you will present yourself in a reasonably good light. Best man speeches can be teasing or risqué, but are usually affectionate. Funeral speeches are nearly always respectful. It could be an interesting exercise to try it again from the point of view of someone who doesn't like you much. You might be one of those fortunate few who have managed to get through life without making enemies, but that is not true for most of us. Most of us have ex-wives, ex-lovers, ex-friends, ex-colleagues who we know would not be all that flattering if they had the chance to write down their true feelings about us. If writing is, as Hemingway said it was, a case of writing 'hard about what hurts', then we should try and put ourselves in the shoes of someone who doesn't share our benign view of ourselves.

Exercise 25

Imagine that someone who you suspect doesn't like you much is writing you a letter about the way you have lived your life. What are they going to say? What will they put in that the funeral orator or best man might leave out? Make notes and then write the letter, trying to capture your former friend's way of speaking. Try and inhabit their mindset as much as possible.

The reason for doing this exercise is to reinforce the obvious point that there are always at least two sides to every story and it's your duty as a biographer or an autobiographer to acknowledge other points of view. However, don't allow the need for balance to cause you to lose focus – you don't want to confuse your readers, and it is absolutely OK to have a strong consistent argument.

Flexibility

Lives are awkward, restless creatures. They simply won't stand still and they resist being encased into a rigid cage no matter how carefully we have designed it. As you research the life, place or period you have decided to write about you will find that your

preconceptions are challenged all the time. Your research may
well lead you off into places where you didn't expect to go. Those
characters you thought might be heroes will turn out to be not quite
as heroic as you had thought, the villains not quite so villainous.
Happy childhoods may turn out to have been miserable all along.
Your own past actions may not stand up to much close scrutiny.

It is in this gap between assumptions and realities that the real
fun of being a creative non-fiction writer lies. It can be unsettling.
But, like a good detective, you have to go wherever the evidence
takes you. This means that your plan must be flexible, adaptable.
You must be able to keep an open mind and to change it when
necessary. It's no good being like the stubborn politician who thinks
they are showing courage when they announce that they are not
for turning, or that they have no reverse gear. A vehicle that can't
turn round or backtrack when circumstances demand it, is more or
less useless. And so is a biographer.

Exercise 26

Here is a little exercise in flexibility. Write down something that
happened to you when you were a child. It doesn't need to be a
big thing. It can be the day you fell off your bike. But when you've
written down the facts as you know them, call up someone else in
your family who might know a little about the incident. Read them
what you've written and ask if they have anything to add. They
almost certainly will. Now rewrite the incident including any new
facts or details you have been given. In any piece of memoir writing
or biography this kind of experience will occur frequently and it
is best to accept new information gracefully and alter your plan,
rather than trying to make it fit your established world-view.

Beginning your research

Personal contacts

With any kind of research-based project the best places to
start are the most obvious. Begin with personal contacts. If it is an

autobiography you are working on then your family and friends will be the first port of call. After this will come teachers, work colleagues, those who knew you as a teammate or a band member, etc. If it is a biography then tell everyone you know what you are working on. I can guarantee that nearly all of them will have contacts of their own, or suggestions of where you should go for information. Some of these – perhaps the majority – will not be relevant but many will be good ideas that will save you much valuable time. You may even find others who are working in a similar field and who have contacts and information that they are willing to share. Certainly, someone who has done something similar recently will have much useful advice to share. Someone who has, say, written a biography of their father who was a submariner during World War II, will have lots to say about how to go about finding the relevant records of your own great-grandfather if he was a sailor during World War I.

Online sources

Most people these days begin any research with the internet. And it is true that search engines have brought a staggering amount of research about almost anything within reach of everyone. And most of it's free too. The trouble is that a lot of it is rubbish.

There's no filter, no quality control. Anyone can say anything they like about anything at all and publish it as fact. Lunatics and fanatics, freaks and weirdos of every shape haunt the alleyways of the internet like a particularly ferocious breed of zombie in a horror flick. There's a lot of seductive nonsense out there and you'll need patience and a highly developed nose for nonsense to avoid being infected by it. Tread carefully and trust nothing on the web unless it comes from unimpeachable sources.

It is, however, getting better. Just as the Wild West was cleaned up as the banks and railroads moved into the lawless frontier towns, so the virtual cities of the web are becoming more orderly. Many of the major libraries – including those of most universities – now have a web presence and you can access their resources from your living room. Likewise, one of your major research tools – the *Dictionary of National Biography* – can be studied via the internet.

In the UK, census returns up to 1911 are also available on the internet now, as are lots of other government records. Churches too – which were for a long time the principal record keepers – have begun to place some of their records online.

Here is a list of some of the websites that you might find most useful in your research:

* A2A – the Access to Archives project – www.a2a.org.uk
   This contains catalogues of numerous archives in England and Wales.

* SCAN – the Scottish Archives Network – www.scan.org.uk
   This aims to provide a single electronic catalogue of the records held in more than 50 Scottish archives. SCAN also aims to make some documents, for example the wills and testaments of Scots from 1500 to 1875, available online.

* NRA – the National Register of Archives – www.hmc.gov.uk.nra
   The NRA is maintained by the Historical Manuscripts Commission and allows searches of a wide range of archives. It covers archive deposits across the UK as well as listing UK material in foreign archives.

* The Church of the Latter Day Saints (Mormons) – www.familysearch.org
   The Mormons place enormous emphasis on genealogy and so have launched a massive project to transcribe all the birth, death and marriage records from around the world. The Church also maintains a number of Family History Centres providing facilities where researchers can study.

* 1911 Census (England and Wales) – www.1911census.co.uk/
   Lots of useful information for those researching the past. Go to www.nationalarchives.gov.uk/records/census-records.htm for information on censuses in England and Wales prior to this date, and www.scotlandspeople.gov.uk/ for censuses in Scotland.

Libraries and public records offices

I love libraries. Quiet places devoted to study and to reading that are free and open to everyone. There is no better index to how civilized a society has become than in the way it funds and values its libraries.

But the best thing about libraries are librarians. Librarians are generally hugely knowledgeable about all manner of subjects, and making friends with the librarian at the one nearest you will save you an enormous amount of time. Remember, every query that you have, big or small, is almost certainly one that they'll have heard and dealt with already. The same is true of public records offices. There is nothing like being led gently through a maze of ancient documentation by someone who knows all the pathways and safe routes out.

Useful tools

Here are some of the most typical forms of material that you will find in a local archive or library that might be most helpful to you:

* Voters' rolls or register of electors

    These provide evidence for residence and evidence of social–economic status. Remember that women didn't get the vote until 1918 (and then it was only for those over 30) and it wasn't until 1928 that they gained full equality with men (votes for all at age 21). Single women got the vote in municipal elections in 1869. The franchise was also restricted for men prior to 1867.

* Valuation rolls

    Very useful for establishing property ownership and, from this, for deducing the social status of an occupant.

* School records

    School logbooks can reveal a great deal about life outside the classroom, the impact of local epidemics being just one example. More obviously, admission registers, reports and school logbooks can provide specific information about this crucial aspect of your subject's childhood development.

* Welfare records

    Included in these records might be the records and logs of workhouses and other forms of relief paid to those who were destitute or unable, through illness or old age, to provide for themselves or their families.

* Local authority records

    These might include the minutes of local authority meetings, as well as documents relating to local planning, health, welfare, education, streets, shops, pavements, etc. Local authorities also maintained the burgess rolls which are very valuable documents for discovering information on people during times of very limited franchise. (Burgesses are, broadly, heads of households with property and a trade, and therefore often had the right to vote.)

* Church records

    These include information not only on births, marriages and deaths but also on education and welfare. In addition many people were employed by the church, and records and accounts can provide valuable information about life in the parish.

* Local newspapers

    Libraries may well have complete back issues of newspapers (including many which no longer exist) and you may find your subject appearing in the pages of their local paper, either in news reports, in the letters columns or as the subject of an obituary.

* Local directories

    These usually consist of an alphabetical listing of property owners and tenants and quite often give the occupations of the householders too. In addition to this information they frequently give details on justices of the peace, local societies and charities, and voluntary bodies.

There is a lot more than this to be found in libraries but the above should give you some sense of how important it is for the creative non-fiction writer to know their way around these places.

Organizing your material

The temptation when you are relying on research is to stick in everything you know about a subject. You will have discovered amazing facts, and a lot of them, and it is natural to want to give as complete a picture as possible. That is, however, not your job. Your job is to make the subject come alive and you can't do that by including everything. You have got to tell a story and to do that you have to work on shaping your material. Just as a sculptor discards most of the clay or bronze he is working with, so much of your information is not going to make it into the main body of your book. The key is to read, summarize and select.

Keeping it legal

There are three basic things to be aware of in keeping a non-fiction book on the right side of the law:

1 copyright
2 permissions
3 acknowledgements.

Copyright exists to protect authors from having their work stolen. If you quote short extracts – a line or two – for educational purposes, then this is usually all right. If you want to quote longer chunks of another writer's work then you will need to get the permission of the copyright holder and there will usually be a fee involved in this. If the writer is dead, copyright on their works will be held by their estate and is usually retained for 70 years after their death. (There are exceptions, and different laws apply in different countries, so do check.)

Copyright exists on letters and legal documents as well as on books and published material, so you will have to gain permission from the owners of these rights too if you wish to quote from them. It is the writer of the letter who owns the copyright **NOT** the receiver. So even if you are the recipient of a hundred letters from a great-aunt vividly detailing her experiences as a spy in World War II you can't publish extracts from them without express permission – and get it in writing – from her or her estate.

Official documents such as birth and marriage certificates are also subject to copyright and this is generally owned by the Crown or the Local Authorities. Again, permission must be sought – and usually paid for – before publication.

Copyright can be a fraught, vexing and tiresome business but it is absolutely essential that you make sure you are covered. It should also go without saying that all material you use should be acknowledged. All sources should be properly credited from the books you have used, all the way to that ten-minute interview you did with Uncle Herb in his retirement home on the Costa Brava.

Writing a proposal

We'll cover more about getting books published in a later chapter, but there are some clear differences between the paths to publication for non-fiction books and for novels and poetry collections that are worth dealing with here.

Unlike novels, non-fiction books are usually sold to publishers on the basis of a proposal and a sample chapter. Most agents and publishers are not – at an early stage with an untried author – going to read a whole manuscript. You need to put together a persuasive proposal. This proposal needs to be short and punchy. But it needs to get across some important information. It needs to tell the editor what your qualifications are for telling this story. So any expertise or experience that you have needs to be flagged up. It also needs to give the publishers or agents some idea of the potential market for the book.

Editors are, quite rightly, interested in projects that will make them money and you need to be aware of this too. You'll need to indicate what other books on this subject exist and what your book will add. If no books exist then that is worth pointing out too. Explain clearly who or what the subject of the book is and why he, she or it is worth writing about.

Remember that your text should be neatly and correctly printed out, double-spaced on one side and not bound or stapled. Do remember to number your pages and have your contact details on your covering letter. You'll find out more about covering letters later on too.

Exercise 27

Write a two-page proposal for a non-fiction subject that you think might interest an editor. It can be for an autobiography, a biography or any other subject. Remember, your aim is simply to intrigue your reader enough that they ask to see more of your work.

This has been a fairly long chapter, but it's a growing area of interest among writers, readers and publishers. I'd like to finish with an exercise adapted from one given to me by the biographers Carole Angier and Sally Cline who, between them, have written ten major biographies including those on Zelda Fitzgerald, Primo Levi and Radclyffe Hall.

Exercise 28

You'll need a partner for this.
1 Interview a friend or a family member (or, even better, another writer) about an event or a relationship in their past. Keep it short; 15 minutes should be plenty of time if you can keep them focused.
2 Write a biographical piece based on the interview. Take no more than 30 minutes to write the piece.
3 Ask your subject to comment on the piece.

The above exercise is very good for showing the differences between biographical and autobiographical writing. It is also very good for showing how much you can accomplish in a short amount of time. It's actually quite a sophisticated exercise, so if it doesn't work out the first time, find a new subject and try it again. It's a particularly good one to try with someone else who wants to write because then you can experience what it is like to be the interviewee. This is an extremely useful thing to have done when you come to interview people for real.

writing for
children

Children are a difficult audience. Not only are there all the competing entertainments in what has become a visual rather than a literary culture, but children are very opinionated about what books they will tolerate never mind like. Generally kids like books that are funny, full of adventure, that feature strong relationships, that are gripping without being too frightening and that end more or less happily. It's a tall order but on the plus side, if a child likes your book then they will love it forever, read it over and over, and seek out anything else you write. Children are a loyal and passionate audience as well as a demanding one. They are honest too. Your adult friends may say nice things about your writing just to be polite. A kid will give it to you straight.

Deciding on an age group

This is your first challenge when writing for children but it is worth thinking about right at the beginning. What is also worth getting right early on is how children at a particular age think and speak. An eight-year-old today may well not talk or even think like an eight-year-old did in 1972. In truth, the fundamentals probably haven't changed all that much, but the language and culture that surrounds today's eight-year-old is very different. It obviously helps if you know some children!

Whatever age you decide to write for, the crucial thing is not to patronize or talk down to your audience. Children want to be talked to on the level.

Exercise 29

When you next visit a bookshop, spend some time in the children's section. Take notice of how the books are arranged. Publishers want to put books into a category. Is it a baby book? For pre-school age? A picture book for children between five and seven years old? Or is it a core fiction, i.e. for 7–12-year-olds? After this you are into 'writing for young adults'. Spend time browsing and reading, rediscovering your own preferences. What are you most drawn to?

If you are uncertain where your own style might fit, try writing a paragraph or two of a story for each age group. Have some books to hand to help with vocabulary and style.

Exercise 30

Spend time with some children. Get them to bring you their favourite books. Read to them, or get them to read to you if they're old enough. Play some games with them, but remember to let them take the lead. The children will be delighted. It's no easy task for even the most winning child to get an adult's close attention. It helps if you've got your own to hand, but grandchildren, nieces, nephews, the kids next door or those at a local school will also appreciate you taking an interest. (Do remember to get proper permission though! If you're going into a school you'll need a Criminal Records Bureau check, which the school can arrange.)

Losing past loves

One of the great things about writing for children is that the books young people fall in love with stay a treasured memory forever. Like childhood itself, a book can often seem even better when seen through the enchanted specs of memory. You will have your own favourites. The Famous Five, The Fantastic Four, Just William, Swallows and Amazons, Molesworth, Biggles, Tracey Beaker, Narnia, The Borrowers and Harry Potter; there's a good chance that you may well have been passionately attached to some of these characters. Well, now you need to let them go. Remember what you liked about them certainly, but don't think that they will come to your aid now. The world is a very different place and children, being infinitely adaptable, are wired for the one they find themselves in.

Exercise 31

Find a passage in a classic children's book that you particularly enjoy and rewrite it in a style that a modern child might appreciate, updating the language and setting as you see fit. Be careful. It's harder than you think to update an acknowledged classic and still make it inspiring and rich.

Originality

Having an original idea that has the legs to sustain an entire book is perhaps the hardest thing in all writing. You might find yourself coming close to despair. All the best ideas for children's fiction can seem like they're already taken. In particular, stories involving toys that come to life, animals with human characteristics and trainee wizards all seem to have been done to death. Nevertheless, themes for children's books are universal and timeless – the secret world, the magical journey, unexpected dangers, being lost, gaining new powers – and original ways of treating these themes are all around you just waiting to be discovered.

In essence all children's stories, from baby books to the most hard-edged, realistic teen fiction, are about making sense of, and expressing wonder at, a big, sometimes frightening world. You need to look at the world as if you were a child as well as a writer. Having access to your childhood self is useful for all writers – Graham Greene described childhood as a writer's capital – but for a writer of young people's fiction it is absolutely essential.

Exercise 32

Take your notebook to a public place – a library is a safe bet but you could try a shopping mall or a sports centre – and make yourself physically small. Sit on the floor and make detailed notes about how it feels to be looking up at everything and everyone.

Giving power to the weak

There is an element of empowering the underdog in all great children's literature. It is unsurprising that children respond particularly well to stories where the weak emerge victorious. However loved and cared for, a child is always living under a dictatorship. The range of decisions they can make is limited. Literature for children should be subversive – a kind of protest song. In books children should make important life-changing decisions; they should have special powers, whether these are supernatural or merely those that result from a keen wit. In other words, children should be at the centre of the world you create. Your universe should be a child's universe.

Of course some of you will be planning worlds where animals are at the centre, or toys or creatures entirely of your own devising. And this is fine. Not only fine, it's great, but I still say that it's the smaller animals, the tiniest creatures, that should come out on top.

Make a list of all the people who have ever done you wrong. Now, think of something that should happen to them. Make it comical if you can. Make it gory, grim and gruesome if you like. Try and make the punishment fit the crime. Revenge is an acceptable motive in all drama and children are very keen on justice. Aim for at least ten and you'll have enough incidents for several children's stories.

Revel in naughtiness

The joy of rudeness

Underpants are always funny. So are bottoms. Children are innocently tickled by the things that adults seem embarrassed by. Aliens that steal underpants, dinosaurs that eat them, people who wear them on their heads. Surreal uses of the everyday and the vulgar will score points with the smaller crowd. Don't be afraid to fart, belch and have stomachs rumble at serious volume.

Your guts for garters

'I'll have your guts for garters' was a favourite phrase of my grandmother's. I didn't understand it, but it sounded deliciously frightening. Exactly the effect that you might want to create in your audience. Children love blood and gore. Adults don't, however (or those reading to young children don't, anyway). And they are at least half your audience. As a responsible writer of children's fiction you should make sure that any violence in your books is there for a reason, that it helps the story along. Yes, we want to frighten our audience a bit. Yes, we want to make them shiver. But we want them to enjoy the thrill of the rollercoaster we're giving them. We don't want them to feel sick and to want to get off. You don't want to terrify young readers.

Think back to the most frightening moment you had as a child. Write it down as plainly and as simply as you can. Now write it down in a way that makes light of the situation somehow. Try writing it as a cartoon, or in rhyme. Or introduce something mad like a purple elephant floating into the story in a hot air balloon. The aim here is to surprise yourself as much as any younger readers.

Extreme characters

Extreme characters are fun to write and children's fiction would seem to be a natural home for them. Especially extremely nasty characters. Roald Dahl is a good example of a writer who isn't constrained by the need to find redeeming features in his characters. In adult fiction people find it difficult to believe in someone who is wholly bad and even harder to enthuse about someone who is wholly good. Our heroes these days must be tainted by flaws which they endeavour to resolve by the end of the book, while our villains often have a reason for their moral turpitude. This isn't necessarily so with characters in children's books and this can be hugely liberating.

I said at the beginning of this book that writing was play, that it should be fun, that essentially it was 'What if...' and 'Let's pretend...', and producing larger than life characters is part of the joy of fiction for kids. Everything can be bigger, brighter, more black and white than would be acceptable in the greyer, more psychologically accurate world of writing for adults.

The problem of problems

Part of the point of reading is to make sense of the world you're in. To try out different ways of being. This is especially important for children who are travelling without maps a lot of the time. When a problem comes up in our lives there is a good chance that we have a storehouse of solutions to draw on. And if not, then there will be places and people we can go to who have the requisite experience. Children often have the choice of blind faith in peers, family or teachers, or trying to work things out on their own. It's a difficult world and being a child is not for the timid. There are real and emotional dangers at every turn. And books, like the best films and the best television, or like a conversation with a good friend, can present children with dilemmas and choices in a safe way. Identifying with the struggles of a character in a book (even if that character is a lonely pig or a homesick dinosaur!) can also be a valuable way for a child to develop empathy and emotional literacy.

Don't preach

But children also hate being lectured. They get enough of being told what to do, so they are naturally resistant to being told what to think. Stories with an obvious didactic intent are likely to be little loved by children, however laudable their aims. It is hard for an author to create a character that engages if that character owes their place on the page to the need to teach the readers a lesson. Children sometimes love their teachers, but they rarely love a teacher's pet. And the characters that are in the book to show us exactly how we should or shouldn't behave are going to be the worst kinds of characters – wooden and lifeless. And we won't trust them.

I began working life teaching drama to troubled children and it seemed that every week we were being encouraged to set up anti-bullying workshops where children would be asked to devise stories around bullying that ended happily. All the children could dream up scenarios where a bully was eventually defeated by defiant kids acting in concert with their noble teachers, but it didn't seem to make much difference to the actual incidence of bullying. The workshops had simply become another lesson with a 'right answer' that had to be given in order to keep 'Sir' happy. Good children's books are driven by conflict and problem-solving but they need surprise, and too many issue-based books lack this essential element.

A good way to make sure that the problems your characters overcome are real is to have the problems arise naturally from their characters. In other words, create the characters in detail so that you know them intimately (this is just as important if your characters are rabbits or moles or rats, or any other creature, real, imagined or mythological!), and the themes, issues and how they deal with them will then come out in an organic, unforced way.

Think of a moral or a message that you consider important for children to learn. Now come up with a short storyline (keep it to one page of A4) that illustrates this, involving two or more characters. Now write detailed character descriptions of those characters. Write down absolutely everything you can think of. Make sure you get in all their likes and dislikes. Now revisit your storyline and inhabit it with the fully rounded characters. Remember: you need to know everything about your character's history. When it comes to the story, however, the readers don't.

Illustrations

Unless you are a very talented artist don't bother doing the drawings for any of your stories yourself. Nor should you get a friend to illustrate them (unless your friend is genuinely gifted in this area). If your story comes to the notice of a publisher they will probably want to choose an illustrator themselves, someone who fits with their house style and who they are used to working with. They've already taken a big chance by accepting your work; it's asking a lot to get them to take on a new illustrator too.

Poetry for children

Children love rhythm and rhyme. They also love alliteration, onomatopoeia, puns and wordplay of all kinds. Part of the joy of writing for children is that exuberant verse finds ready appreciation. Clever or outrageous rhymes and vivid imagery as well as a gripping narrative can greatly endear a book to a child. You don't want to make it too obvious however. You want to pile surprise on surprise for your audience. In general a good rule is to go for the third rhyme that you think of. The first is one that children might think of for themselves. The second is one that their parents will think of. The third rhyme that occurs to you may be the original, startling one that delights. It may also be the word that prompts you to take your story in directions that surprise even you, the writer.

Sharing stories

Remember, children aren't the same as us. They are not cynical or distrustful. They expect to be liked and admired. They expect that people will find their stories fascinating and in return they expect that you are a nice, friendly entertaining person with a fund of stories of your own. And they are right. Spend time with children and you will want to make yourself worthy of their trust in you. And you will want your stories to be treasured too and you will work hard to make them as good as they can be because this audience really does deserve the best of you.

Exercise 36

Write a story for your chosen age group. Spend as much time on it as you would on a story for adults. Read it aloud to yourself. Put it away for a while, then redraft it. Then put it away again and redraft it again. Get a candid constructive reader friend to make suggestions. Redraft it again. Now get a child of the right age group to read it. Make any more necessary changes. Now comes the crucial test: read it to a small group of the right age group at a nearby school or youth group (get all the proper authorities to agree through all the right channels). Elicit their honest reactions and solicit suggestions for how it could be improved. As with any advice you are free to ignore it. Some of it will be contradictory anyway, but what you can't ignore is the feeling in the room. That never lies. You will be able to tell if your story is holding the attention of its target audience. However well-behaved your audience, if their concentration is faltering then rustlings, fidgetings and whisperings will let you know. Even if the kids are silent there will be something about the dead quality of the air that will tell you which parts have failed to grab them. Similarly, the atmosphere will become subtly charged if your story is doing its job.

Some writers are better readers and performers than others. If you are not a natural performer it really is worth putting the hours in and improving. It is something you can learn with practice and repetition.

7

starting to write a novel

There are literally a million manuscripts in the offices of literary agents in London and New York at any one time. Only a fraction of these get published. Don't let that put you off however. None of these novels is your novel. None of them are written with your voice. None of them say what only you can say. The novel is a long, long journey and like any major trip your chances of success are massively increased if you plan and prepare properly.

Done properly writing a novel can be the trip of a lifetime. As you move through the jungles, seas, deserts, and cities of your imagination you are Shackleton, Amundsen, Scott, Armstrong, Livingstone, Columbus, Captain Cook, Ellen MacArthur, Amy Johnson and Nelson Mandela. You are a statesman-explorer and you don't even have to leave your living room.

The challenge

Of all the courses I have organized over the years, those that deal with novel-writing are the most in demand. If, after tackling the exercises that follow, you don't want to write novels, then I still believe that you have completed an important part of a writer's journey. That is, deciding what kind of writer you are. In any case, I'm not sure that I believe you. As far as I can tell all playwrights, screenwriters, journalists, children's writers and bloggers still want to pit themselves against the challenge of writing a novel. Only some poets – and perhaps some short story writers – seem immune to this siren call.

First steps

A literary novel is between 70,000 and 200,000 words, with most coming in at about 100,000. Before starting down this long road you need to decide what kind of book you are going to write. I don't simply mean what genre are you going to write in – crime, historical, romantic, science or literary fiction – but what is your book going to be about? And why does it need to be written?

Exercise 37

In not more than 100 words, write down exactly why you want to write a novel and who you hope will read it. This will help clarify in your mind your aims and objectives.

The theme

What is your story going to be about? This is a single word or a short phrase that encapsulates the essence of the story. Being clear about this right at the outset, before you've thought about plot, setting or characters, will help you stay focused and prevent your novel becoming a sprawling mess. It will prevent you being led off at tangents and into cul-de-sacs. It will, with any luck, save you time later when it comes to editing (it probably won't but you can always hope). Dianne Doubtfire put it well when she said that 'A book without a theme can become a mere sequence of events with no foundation, no reason for existence.'

Your theme will probably be something that you have personal experience of. A passionate desire to communicate experience and knowledge will give your book an inner heat, a propulsive motor that will keep it going.

But a novel is not an autobiography and having your theme shining ahead of you as you write will help you cut out those parts of your life story that don't fit. It will also help as a reminder to make sure that you alter details of your life as you need to. Like a good tabloid editor, you mustn't let the facts get in the way of a good story. As I've said before, 'Write what you know' is good advice for a writer but so is its opposite: 'Write what you don't know' – this can be important too. Making stuff up is part of a fiction writer's job and one you shouldn't shy away from. One important difference between fictive lives and our own lives is that in fiction everything has to mean something. This is often not the case in real life.

Exercise 38

Write down five themes that you feel qualified to tackle. Now circle two of these as contenders for the theme of your first book.

Viewpoints

Conventional wisdom has it that the easiest kind of book to write is one with an omniscient third-person narrator. A God figure able to see into the minds of all the characters and able to follow them all. I disagree. I like a limited narrator who only has access to parts of the story. As a new novelist I would be inclined to keep things simple. Match ambition to your limited experience. Admittedly, this will give you some problems later on because you can only tell the reader things that your narrator would know. You can only get to know the characters through him or her. But this very straitjacket forces you to keep things tightly focused.

Multiple narrators

Readers' attention will flag a little when a narrator takes over who they don't warm to. This happens even in great books like Jonathan Franzen's *The Corrections* or Irvine Welsh's *Trainspotting*, both of which are first-person novels told by more than one character. Great novels, great voices, but still some narrators appeal more than others.

My own first novel, *Tag*, is narrated in turn by a 40-year-old male high school teacher and a 15-year-old girl who is a working-class tearaway. People seemed to like both voices but nearly everyone preferred the voice of Colleen, my feisty hooligan. Bafflingly, they also thought Colleen's voice rang the most true. Obviously my inner teenage girl had been desperate to be let out for years and so she seized the chance when she got it. Jonathan Diamond, my other narrator, was maybe slightly slower off the mark. This is another reminder of how important it can be not to be too hamstrung by sticking solely to what you know when beginning your book. Observation and empathy will take you a long way.

Whose story is it?

There is a saying that 'character is story'. It is the characters that will drive your plot. But not all characters will have equal weight. Your novel is not a democracy. Even if you decide to write in the third person you will still need to have a central character in whom the readers can invest their emotional energy. Even if this central character is unlikeable, evil even, we want to see the world through their eyes.

Exercise 39

Keeping your theme in mind, write brief character sketches for six of your principal characters (any more than six major characters and you risk losing control of them entirely). Now who, out of this collection, deserves to be the central character? Who is going to be the hero of this book? Choose carefully because this person is going to stay with you night and day for months or years. They are going to have to be fascinating to you now, and grow more fascinating as the story develops. Having the wrong central character is probably what prevents first novels getting off the ground more than almost any other fault (except, possibly, over-ambition).

The voice

Finding the voice of your central character is key to unlocking the story. A strong, engaging voice propels the storyline and hooks the reader in: Rob, the melancholy music obsessive in Nick Hornby's *High Fidelity*; Judith Bastiaanz, the naïve young Dutch émigré to the New World whose disastrous first infatuation helps destroy her family in Kathryn Heyman's *The Accomplice*; the dizzy but determined Bridget in Helen Fielding's *Bridget Jones's Diary*; Holden Caulfield in J. D. Salinger's *Catcher in the Rye*, the prototype of every moody teenage narrator we have had since the 1950s (Caulfield's direct descendant is the unlucky Vernon in D. B. C. Pierre's Booker Prize-winning *Vernon God Little*); Bessy Buckley, the wide-eyed, sassy nineteenth-century hero in Jane Harris's *The Observations* has a rollicking voice that carries the whole novel; Christopher, the maths prodigy with Asperger's Syndrome in Mark Haddon's groundbreaking *The Curious Incident of the Dog in the Night-time*; the earnest and wise Scout in *To Kill A Mockingbird*. All of these strike me as good examples of stories where a strong narrative voice has been established right at the beginning of the book and sustained through to the end. There are countless others, however. All of the characters mentioned above have flaws (except just possibly the child, Scout) but none of them are unlikeable. Holden Caulfield can seem alienated and difficult but that is exactly why he exercises such a pull on the psyche of generations of teenagers.

The point is that these narrators have a voice which is vivid, alive and unique. They all share the fact that they look at the world in unusual, albeit very different ways.

Voice is probably the hardest of skills to master. It is certainly the hardest to explain, which is why I've reached for so many different examples. It's important to get it right. A wrong note in the voice of your narrator and you will quickly begin to lose the trust of your readership.

Even if you have made the decision to write your book in the third person, you will still need to have a voice. An invisible narrator is actually impossible: readers will be responding to a narrative voice whether or not it is that of an actual character. Voice in this context may be a synonym for style. Look at the novels of Fay Weldon or E. L. Doctorow to see how the third-person novel still requires the push of a powerful narrative voice.

Exercise 40

Experiment with the voices of your central characters. Have each of them recount an incident from their childhood in their own words. This will be a good way to test whether or not your central character is the right one. Try and make their voices as distinct from each other as you can.

Structure

Aspiring writers worry about structure more than they worry about anything else. It's as though the word 'structure' holds the same sense of arcane unknowable magic as the words 'quantum physics'. And yet the mechanics of story structure are relatively straightforward. Most books, plays, films and television dramas are written with a three act structure. And this phrase in itself seems to be a posh way of saying: Beginning, Middle and End.

Three acts, three kinds of plot

The plot is the journey of your characters through these three acts. There are, essentially, three kinds of plot. The first is the most familiar.

The linear plot

A linear plot is where the action moves straightforwardly through the acts, the tension building until a climax in the final act.

This kind of plotting is familiar to us from many an action movie, as well as many classic novels.

The other two kinds of plot are cyclic. In other words the position at the end of the book resembles that at the start, except that all the characters are utterly changed.

The heroic cycle

Familiar to us from the great epics such as *King Arthur* or *The Odyssey*, this follows the pattern of: Departure, Initiation and Return (think of the structure of *The Hobbit*).

The mythic journey

This can be expressed as: Cage, Escape, Quest, Dragon and Home (think of the structure of *Watership Down* – warned by a vision of impending catastrophe a group of young rabbits decide to leave their threatened warren (Cage); they get away despite the best and brutal efforts of the authorities to stop them (Escape); they then search for exactly the right place to set up a new warren (Quest), defeating the fearsome Nazi warren run by General Woundwort (Dragon); finally they end their days in bounty, together with the does they liberated from the enemy warren (Home).

Another way of thinking about this kind of structure might be as three acts containing five parts, these parts being: Inciting incident, Complication, Betrayal, Climax and Resolution. Act One would contain the Inciting incident and the Complication, things heat up with a Betrayal in Act Two, and Act Three would contain the Climax but also the Resolution.

Exercise 41

Take your central character on a journey using one or more of the plot types described above. What type is going to best suit your theme? Just sketch it out for now.

Setting

This is where your novel takes place and when. It is worth thinking a little about this right at the planning stage of your novel.

> You have a theme and a collection of characters and a rough idea of
> the type of journey that they might undertake. You might want to
> jot down now the kind of locations where scenes might take place.

Get your facts straight

You will want to choose the kinds of settings that you yourself
know well. If you know Edinburgh and you know council offices
then utilize this knowledge. Likewise if you know college radio
stations and you know Berkeley then utilize that knowledge too.
The reader will want to trust that you know what you're talking
about. The same is true of historical periods: if you are writing
a novel about the past then you owe it to your readers to have
researched thoroughly the time in which your book is set. This is
true even if you lived through the era about which you are writing.
The memory is an unreliable muscle and you will need to go and
check your facts. Make sure that you have the right prime minister
in power, or that people really were sending emails in 1993.

You will also want to avoid clichés about historical periods.
For example a cliché about the 1980s is that it was all Gordon Gecko
and Greed is Good, with the whole nation in thrall to earning money
at the expense of everybody else. And yet what I remember from
the 1980s is the dole, the *Socialist Worker* sellers at tube stations,
the first appearance of beggars on British streets in hundreds of
years, and strikes. Nobody I knew was wearing braces and making
a killing on the stock market.

In a similar way the 1960s is often portrayed as the decade of
free love and explosive social change. And for an elite that might
have been true. But for most people the sexual liberation didn't
happen until later as the changes in social mores only gradually
filtered out from London and the West Coast of the USA.

Time periods

Another big decision to make is over what time period your
story is going to unfold. Is it over decades, as with the classic great

American novels like *The World According To Garp*? Or is it just one day, like James Joyce's *Ulysses* or Ian McEwan's *Saturday*?

Whatever you decide, thinking about how the weather changes and how the seasons affect the lives of your characters will help give you a sense of how your story might unfold. Farmers are perhaps the most affected by these kinds of changes, but shopkeepers must plan for Christmas and Halloween. School teachers plan for examination periods. Everyone is affected by the nights drawing in and the weather getting colder and wetter. In India, or America, or Africa, the seasons are different and will affect your characters in different ways. The rhythm of the world they inhabit must impact on your characters in some way.

Teach something

For many, part of the pleasure of reading novels is learning. In a great novel one will learn about the world, about human nature, about oneself and about different time periods. But there are other more low-key pleasures to be had. The novels of John Murray teach about contemporary Cumbria, a place to which, shamefully, I have never been; *The Electric Michelangelo* by Sarah Hall is fascinating on the evolution of tattooing; the novels of George Macdonald Fraser are the best kind of historical writing, with painstakingly researched facts set in the context of exhilarating action; *Trainspotting* is fascinating on the world of Scottish junkies; while Nicholas Royle's *Antwerp* brings to vivid life the demi-monde of a city which no one outside of Belgium knows very much about.

If you have special knowledge about something, whether it is breeding pedigree cats or manufacturing class A drugs, then I suggest that giving the readers access to this kind of information is actually a kind of generosity.

Story, story, story

It often comes as something of a shock to those who attend writing courses that 80,000 beautiful words do not make a novel.

I have said that your characters generate the story and this is true. But you are not writing lengthy character studies. There must be constant movement, ceaseless surprising progressions. Just as much modern music now seeks to wring the maximum out of each chord before moving a tune forward, thus sacrificing melody and urgency, so many emerging novelists forget that what keeps us turning pages is a story.

Novelists, even the most serious ones, are in the entertainment business. We are purveyors of pleasure as well as knowledge. It is a complicated, complex kind of pleasure but pleasure nevertheless. Ford Madox Ford wrote that each line of the novel should push it forward. Things have to happen, your characters need to make things happen and then respond to things that other characters do and say. They can't stand still and they shouldn't reflect for too long or too often, unless reflecting for too long is part of their essence in which case it should have troubling consequences for them. A novel is a sophisticated form of fairground. In the hands of a good novelist you should get the visceral thrills of the rollercoaster, combined with the darker arts of the illusionist. Things have to happen.

Don't get it right, get it written

I don't know who said this first. It is excellent advice for those starting out on the journey of the novel, however. Too many new writers begin their first chapter in the white heat of creativity and then polish and hone and tweak that opening over and over until it's shining. In the meantime months have passed and the momentum of the story has been lost.

Bash it down; get it on the page. Forget the critic on your shoulder who has tried to stop you doing anything worthwhile since you were born, and is not helpful at this stage in your life. You will go back and edit and change and tweak and redraft and suffer all the agonies associated with that stage, but for now you need to draw up a realistic schedule for blasting out that first draft. Let it burst out without worrying about coherence or structure or spelling or paragraphing. Get it done. Get it out of you. The real work of the novelist begins with the redrafting. As the poet David Harsent says, 'All writing is rewriting.' Nevertheless, a bit of planning will help you put your first draft down with minimal risk of becoming blocked.

Exercise 43

You're serious about writing a novel so draw up a plan of campaign. Set yourself a deadline. Think about how long you've got to write this novel. You'll need time to plot, time to develop your characters, time to work on the setting, time to write a synopsis and then you'll need to write a first draft. And of course you'll need time to do all the other things in your life – work, family, exercise. Writing your novel shouldn't cost you any of these, that's too high a price to pay.

Of course you should have a writing routine established by now. Break the task of getting this novel down into chunks and stick to the schedule you've set yourself, whether that is six weeks of planning, followed by a chapter a week, or another schedule which is manageable for you. Write it on the calendar and pin it somewhere prominent.

This chapter has been about starts and springboards. If all has gone to plan then you should be ready to begin a first chapter.

Exercise 44

Write the first chapter of your novel. Don't give everything away at once. Remember what Charles Reade wrote in his nineteenth-century writing manual *Advice to young authors on writing novels*, 'Make 'em laugh; make 'em cry; make 'em wait.'

8

the difficult business of second drafts

All writing is rewriting. No one ever finished writing their first draft, posted it off and sat back to receive the applause and the cheques.

'The first draft of anything is shit' said Hemingway, but he should have added that they are necessary shit. I'm a real believer in spewing out a first draft, leaving it to ferment or compost for a while and then going over it systematically and ruthlessly. Be your own harshest critic. The chances are you'll need to revise everything. If you've left enough time between drafts, new and better ideas will have occurred to you already. And it's amazing how the composting process will have revealed exactly the cuts you need to make in order for your final project to be the best it can be.

And remember, however short your piece is – it is still too long.

When you embark on the rewriting process the first thing is to read your work very carefully. You'll need to know your novel inside out. And don't read it on the computer. Make sure you have a hard copy printed double-spaced with a wide margin, so that you can scribble notes and revise phrases. There is something about having real paper in your hand that enables you to spot mistakes much, much more easily than when they are on the screen. New ideas will occur to you all the time as you read your manuscript and I promise that the craft of revision, which seemed so painful when you began, will quickly begin to create its own exhilarating energy. When you first contemplate revising a book it can seem like climbing the same hard, high mountain all over again without even the thrill of conquering it to look forward to. You've already seen the view from the summit, you've already had the triumphant glow of having achieved the top. Surely doing it again just gives you the slog without the joy? Fortunately, though there are numerous similarities between writing and mountain-climbing, they are not an exact match.

As you progress through your redraft you will find new routes, new views, new and better ways to express yourself. Your copy of your text will become covered in scribbles and crossings out and hieroglyphs that will mean nothing to you but are your blueprint for the book you were always meant to write.

There will also be times when you smile at your work.

When not to murder your babies

In 1914 in *On the Art of Writing*, Sir Arthur Quiller-Couch wrote:

> **Whenever you feel an impulse to perpetrate a piece of exceptionally fine writing, obey it – wholeheartedly – and delete it before sending your manuscript to press. Murder your darlings.**

This is crazy, isn't it? Joe Orton said that whenever he came across a piece in his own work that made him laugh out loud, then that is what he would end up cutting. More fool him. Writing is so often difficult and painful that it seems perverse to make it harder than it needs to be. You started writing because there were things only you could say. And because you felt you had a unique way of saying them. Why cut what makes your work special? Why stop doing the thing that you do best? No one thought it was a good idea to put George Best in goal; no one puts the marathon runner Paula Radcliffe in for the 100-metre sprint. Of course we have to be alert for work that seems pretentious. And some of your work which seems especially fine on a first or second reading will seem awkward in a third draft when everything around it has changed. But in this context *don't* kill your babies, nurture them, work on them, improve on them. These stylistic tics may be the very things future readers cherish about your work.

Exercise 45

Give yourself a tick every time you come across something in your work that you really really like. Don't cheat, you have to genuinely love it. Then count your ticks. Do the same exercise after a redraft; with any luck the number has gone up significantly. You are doing this as a confidence boost. You are a good writer, stick at it.

Working preferences

I suggested that you write in scenes, and you should revise the same way. Does every scene deserve its place in the piece as a whole and does each sentence within the scene need to be there?

Some writers feel the need to perfect each sentence as far as possible before going on to the next. This is fine. Many of the best writers work this way. I don't. I believe in roughing the work out in full and going back. Others will write out a thousand words in rough in the morning and then edit and revise those words in the afternoon. There are nearly as many working methods as there are writers and there's certainly no right way to go about it. However, you should beware of honing one particular area of your work so much that it holds you up and you never finish. That's the literary equivalent of pruning your hanging baskets while the garden quietly turns into a jungle.

A lot of new writers have a fantastically polished first chapter and struggle to complete the whole book. Good enough is sometimes good enough.

What all writers should be wary of is just revising on the computer screen. The edit tools are very seductive. The urge to spend all day cutting, pasting and rearranging the text can get in the way of actually doing any writing. It is easy to convince yourself that you are writing when you are in fact simply typing.

Points for revision

1 Have you begun in the right place?

A lot of novice writers find themselves apologizing to those kind people who have volunteered to be the first readers of a work – 'The story doesn't really get going until chapter three' they stammer. In which case, chapter three should actually be the first chapter. Amazingly, similar apologies crop up in the covering letters sent with submissions to agents and publishers.

There is also that tendency among new writers to give too much away in the first chapter. However, you should aim to grab the reader in the opening passages, whatever genre you are writing in.

2 Is there too much back story?

There might well be information about your characters that you need to know but the reader doesn't. We have considered many different ways of creating fully rounded characters, but some of this should inform you as you write, rather than be for the reader to plough through.

3 Are there any unintentional repetitions?

The answer is almost certainly yes. When you are writing at speed and in the heat of inspiration, this is understandable. So revise with care, eliminating all the words which could undermine the flow of your prose. A more difficult problem to eradicate might be where you have repeated ideas rather than phrases. It is easy to say the same thing twice, in different ways.

4 Is anything irrelevant?

Have you included material which is not related to your central theme? The first draft of my first book certainly included a great deal that had personal resonance for me, but which was unnecessary in terms of my plot. It all had to go.

5 Is your research showing?

This is a particular danger for non-fiction writers, but novelists can suffer from it too. As you get ready to write a book your reading and trawling through the weirder, wilder reaches of Google will have unearthed all sorts of arcane facts that you'll be tempted to crowbar into your book. Don't. Stories are wiry, tough creatures but they can still be crushed beneath a weight of unnecessary research. Your reader may become frustrated trying to wade through the maze you have created for them. They may give up. The trivial pursuits champion at a dinner party, who knows a million facts about every subject that comes up in conversation, may be nice, clever and widely read, yet also unlikely to ever get a girlfriend. In the same way your book too may find itself a wallflower in the library through inflicting too much unnecessary knowledge upon the reader.

6 Is there any dead wood?

One writer I know sets his students this exercise: they must write for 30 minutes on a set subject and then they must cut every other word. Sometimes the result is gobbledygook, but often individual sentences and paragraphs are improved in surprising ways. Cutting the dead wood is the very essence of good writing. Get rid of whatever is superfluous. Slash and burn. Be ruthless. My hard drive contains 100,000 words of my first book that were never used. The result of four complete drafts. And how do you spot the dead wood? If you have let your manuscript simmer in a drawer, away from prying eyes and sunlight for a good long while, then dead wood will leap out at you. More dead wood will become apparent if you read the work out loud. Also, every sentence over 30 words is almost certainly too long.

If you have spent as much time on revising as you did on writing the book in the first place, you might be tempted to think that *now* it is finished. It must be. Well, put it away for another few days and come back to it again. There will still be too many words. And when your candid friends have given it the once over, there will still be more to cut.

There will still be material that embarrasses you whenever you think of it.

The art of good style

The point of getting rid of all the clutter is to highlight your style, not to obscure it. If you write in your own way, and do it regularly, you will establish a style which you feel comfortable with. Cutting will be part of the process of clearing all that doesn't fit with your style or your strategy.

Study excellence

One of the great things about becoming a serious writer is that you become a very serious reader. Every book you read from now on will have lessons for you; every facet of that book will have heightened resonance for you. Reading will still be an enjoyable entertainment, but it will be more than that.

Every author will be a tutor, every story a guide for your own work. This is not to say that you should copy other writers, though actually of course you should. Sometimes writers say that they don't read while they are writing in case another writer's style rubs off. To me that would seem to be the point.

Guitarists watch the hands of other players in order to spot new chord shapes and tricks of technique. Artists can become incredibly learned about the techniques of creating colour from the eighteenth century. Knowing all you can about your chosen craft gives you more options in your own writing. You should stay open-minded to writers whose taste is not your own, whose politics are not your own, whose subject matter you might find distasteful. You don't need to be a lesbian to enjoy the strong characters, heady atmospherics and powerfully plotted novels of Sarah Waters, for example.

You should also read contemporary work wherever possible. The world has moved on since the books you studied in high school. If you are serious about writing you need to know what is happening now, as well as the masters of the past. Literature is a fashion-conscious business just like any other, and tastes change.

The enemies of good style

Cliché

A cliché is a phrase that has become stale with overuse: 'weak at the knees', 'over the moon', 'white as a sheet'. As *The New Fowler's Modern English Usage* reminds us, the word cliché has 'come to be applied to commonplace things of other kinds – visual images, stock situations, remarks in radio and television (and now, if you'll excuse me I've got work to do), ideas and attitudes etc'.

You should also avoid clichéd situations: the husband who arrives home from work unexpectedly to find his wife in the arms of another man; the suicide note on the mantelpiece. Dianne Doubtfire put it well when she said, 'Good style has a lot to do with freshness of vision.' My personal pet hate among clichés is where someone seems to vomit noisily as they come across a dead body. I'm sure this happens sometimes, but in literature, theatre and television it happens all the time and in the same kind of ways.

Sentimentality

This is normally caused by over-writing a powerful scene which involves a character you care for. It's easily done when that character is facing a moment of acute crisis. Read these passages with a stony heart, and be particularly receptive to criticisms that any early readers may have about these passages. As Carl Jung put it, 'Sentimentality is a superstructure covering brutality.'

Clumsy phrases

These are phrases which can jerk readers from the world you are constructing for them into the real world. Something irritates. Reading out loud any phrases you suspect might be awkward will be the final test. Speaking the words out loud will also help you find your way to a better way of putting things.

Too many adjectives and adverbs

The most common, but most easily corrected of all the mistakes beginners make, is to overuse adjectives and adverbs. Adverbs also tend to be the mark of lazy writing, telling us what someone thinks or feels rather than showing us. Adjectives have a dulling effect on a piece of prose, limiting the reader's own imagination and suggesting a lack of confidence on the part of the writer. It engenders a feeling that they can't quite manage to describe a person or event properly. It makes readers feel that they are not in safe hands: that the pilot doesn't quite know how to fly the plane.

Exercise 46

Write a descriptive piece of 300 words or so, using no adjectives or adverbs. When the work is finished you may add one of each.

Exercise 47

Now imagine that you have been asked to turn that 300-word description into a 200-word piece for an anthology of new writing.

Poor punctuation

It's not really the role of this book to teach you about punctuation – for that you need Lynne Truss's excellent *Eats, Shoots and Leaves* – but you should be aware that editors will not correct incoherent grammar or punctuation, they will merely assume that you don't know what you're doing. In particular, be careful to use colons and semicolons correctly.

agents
and
publishers

The slush pile. This is a filing cabinet full of manuscripts in a publisher's office that await the attentions of a 17-year-old intern who might, if you are lucky, pass your book on upwards if they feel it has any merit. The intern (let's call her Felicity, for that is almost certainly her name) might be a gifted and perceptive reader, but she is also likely to be very busy answering the phone, ordering paper for the photocopier and fetching three bean wraps for the lunches of more senior executives. Your book might not get Felicity's full attention.

Just sticking your book, however brilliant, into a jiffy bag and punting it off to publishers is the equivalent of turning up on a date late, scruffy, unwashed and skint. It shows a lack of respect to the industry and towards your own work.

What happens when you've written your book? The reality is that if you simply send your manuscript off to a publisher you will be placed on the slush pile. In the first instance what you need to do is find an agent.

Why do you need an agent?

Having a good agent is like having a native guide through hostile territory. A good agent is not a counsellor, a social worker, a teacher, an editor, a lawyer, an expert in industrial relations or a psychotherapist, though at times they might seem like all these things. A good agent is your champion in the publishing world. For 10 or 15 per cent of your earnings, they will try and find the most suitable editor at the publisher best placed to promote your work well.

Having found a publisher they will negotiate fees, often including fees for audio books, film rights and foreign sales. And before all this they often do the work that editors used to do but don't really any more. A skilful agent reads your work for its literary merit, but also with their knowledge of the current marketplace. They will make suggestions for ways to improve your manuscript, which are usually worth following. Bear in mind that they like your writing – that's why they took you on in the first place – so what they have to say about your book is made with your best interests as a writer at heart.

The trouble is – like any really good things – they can be hard to find.

Having an agent is doubly useful because publishers use them as a filter. If you have succeeded in convincing an agent that there is potential in your book, then publishers are much more likely to take notice.

How do you get an agent?

You want an agent who is going to be sympathetic to your work so it is worth doing some research. First-time novelists will always thank their agents somewhere on the book, so if you have read a first novel you have enjoyed and whose work seems to be in a similar area to yours, then that agent might be a possibility. Use the internet to find out which established writers agents represent. Agents often give talks at literary festivals, so go along and hear what they have to say. Many – most – agents will have a lot of clients that they are already looking after and may just be too busy to give you the attention your work needs. They may not be simply giving you the brush off when they say that their lists are full.

When you have a list of potential agents don't send them the whole manuscript. Send them the first 60 pages of your book, together with a polite, short covering letter. If they like the opening pages then they'll ask for the rest. Send your pages in a proper jiffy bag. Don't use one of those made from recycled cardboard that will explode in a cloud of grey chaff when your would-be agent tears it open. If you have just ruined a favourite outfit then the agent is unlikely to look upon your work as favourably as they might have done otherwise.

Don't send a synopsis. This is controversial advice, I know. Lots of other people will say you should always send one. What's the point? If they don't like the first 60 pages, they are unlikely to say to themselves, 'but look how it ends'! If they like the pages they'll read the whole book anyway.

Send your work to several agents simultaneously. Again, controversial advice but it means that if one agent rings you up asking to meet, then you can call the others, saying that you are having a meeting with Agent X and could you perhaps meet them too? At the very least this will ensure that they read your work pretty quickly.

When to contact an agent

It is best to wait until you have finished your book and got it into its best possible shape. This means at least a second, possibly even a third, full draft. If an agent accepts you on the strength of 60 brilliant pages, and the rest of the book is theoretical at this stage, misunderstandings can occur. The book you eventually produce might well be some distance from the book the agent thought you were producing. Cue disappointment all round.

The covering letter

This should be short, polite and employ judicious use of flattery, 'I've heard that you are a fantastic agent and you represent X whose work I very much admire...'. Don't write too much about yourself, just that which is interesting. Don't mention your job unless it's a very interesting one or relevant to the book. You are selling yourself as well as the work. Do mention any courses you've taken, such as those with the Arvon Foundation. Mention too any successes you have had with writing, prizes won or stories published. If you have a track record then let them know. Don't forget to include your contact details.

Send your letter to a named agent. Simply sending it to the agency will mean that it could end up anywhere, including on the desk of the newest intern. You can follow up with a phone call but wait at least a few weeks before you do this.

Exercise 48

Write a practice covering letter. Make sure that you get it proofread by a competent, literate friend.

Meeting agents

You should, if you get the chance, shop around for agents. I suppose, I didn't. The first agent I approached agreed to take me on and I was thrilled. I had met her once before at a literary event and knew already that she was razor-sharp, hard-working, thoughtful and passionate about books. She is also incredibly personable, which is important to me. It might not be to you. I have a writer friend who prizes his agent because she is, in his words 'a Rottweiler', a notorious terrorizer of publishers who generally plays hardball in every aspect of her life. I can see why you might want that in an agent. It's not for me though. I like to be able to have a laugh with my agent.

And her comments on my work have always been astute and her dealings with the business end of things more than professional. This is not to say that I have always taken her advice. But on those occasions when I've trusted my judgement rather than hers, I have always, always been wrong. She has never said 'I told you so' even though she could have. I wouldn't have blamed her.

Not all agents are as good as this. Anyone can set themselves up as an agent, which is another reason for doing your research first. Know who else they represent and meet them in their offices to decide whether you can trust them.

Publishers

If you keep writing for any length of time you will begin to hear a lot of moaning about publishers. Some of it is justified. However, one thing that should keep you from falling prey to a debilitating despair is the fact that writers have *always* been complaining about the publishing industry.

It is true that publishers face some difficult times. Reading as a leisure pursuit is in decline, squeezed by the plethora of noisier alternatives. The big bookselling chains and the supermarkets demand huge discounts which eat into publishers', already small, profit margin.

Books have a much shorter shelf-life than they once did. If the book doesn't shift copies in the first few weeks, then it is off the shelves and heading back to the warehouse. The carefully crafted books that take a year of agony to write are less in demand than ever before. Instead the ghosted celebrity memoir, fitness bibles, cookbooks and television tie-ins dominate.

Small cogs in a big machine

Authors are so many cogs in a machine producing units for mass consumption, and if the masses don't want a serious volume of the units you produce, then let's get somebody else in. Let's try and turn another – preferably young and good-looking – writer into a brand. Better still, let's find an established young and good-looking brand – a pop star or a footballer's girlfriend – and see if we can squeeze some units out of that.

The independent bookshops are all closing, Amazon is selling books with huge discounts, Tesco and Walmart sell them for still less and even libraries have become internet cafés where the loaning out of books is just a sideline to their real business of helping the long-term unemployed brush up their computer skills. All this and worse is what you'll hear and there's some truth to it.

It seems that in the old days writers were allowed to grow and develop, to build a following. Publishers would keep faith with an author over several books, not necessarily making money until quite late on in a writer's career. Not now. These days instant returns are demanded. And even if those instant returns are achieved then they must be equalled with the next book. Even well-established authors live in fear of their books being rejected.

Despite this, publishing houses, like literary agencies, are staffed by people who love books. Really love books, to the point of being obsessed by them. In fact, more books are published in the UK than ever before. The industry still makes money.

Fresh talent

And publishers still want to find the next big thing. As a new writer you do have one huge advantage over the competition. You are a fresh voice. You are offering something different. If you are a writer on your fourth novel and the last three sold, say, 5,000 each, your publisher could be forgiven for thinking that this one too will sell 5,000 copies. Why should the writer suddenly sell millions now? Whereas a new voice might just catch hold of the public imagination and make mega-bucks for all concerned. The publishing industry needs new writers or there's no industry at all. And yes, of course they are tempted to invest in the young and good-looking, but there are plenty of inspiring stories about older first-time writers. Marina Lewycka (*A Short History of Tractors in Ukrainian*), Alice Sebold (*The Lovely Bones*) and Mary Wesley (*The Camomile Lawn*) had been writing unsuccessfully for years before they were picked up and became household names.

There are still some very big advances being offered to writers. You'll have no doubt read about those in six figures, but these headline figures don't generally stand up to too much scrutiny. Say a writer gets £100,000 ($150,000), this might well be for three books with just one-third paid upon signing. The rest of the money is paid as further books are delivered.

If each book takes, on average, two years from first idea to first print run, then that is actually slightly less than £17,000 ($25,000) per year, a figure which actually compares rather badly with being a nurse or a teacher. And that's for a huge advance; most are much smaller. The average advance for a first novel is about £3,000 ($4,500). J. K. Rowling's first advance was £1,500 ($2,250) paid in two instalments. And if a writer gets a huge advance, then they need huge sales. Should those sales not be forthcoming then they are likely to be dumped with very little ceremony. And who wants to be an ex-novelist?

Some people make a lot of money from books. But I guess it won't be us, not yet anyway. Generally the more a publisher pays for a book, the more they will invest in promoting a book. Authors don't want the big advances just because they're greedy but because they want a publisher to get behind their book with advertising and promotion. Publishers that have invested a lot of hard cash will energize their sales teams; will organize special events; will make sure your books are visible in the shops. (They do this by paying for display space. Independent bookshops will put whoever they want in the window or in prominent piles in the shop. The big chains have sold this space to publishers.)

Small presses

It is true that there are fewer mainstream publishers than ever before (many of the imprints turn out to be owned by the same company), but changes in the printing and distribution industry have meant that there are a lot (really a lot) of small presses, many with very good reputations, which succeed in developing the careers of their writers. Some of these writers are happy to stay with the publishers who discovered them, others move up to the bigger league.

A lot of independent publishers are kitchen table affairs. Book enthusiasts trying to publish half a dozen titles on a shoestring. These are people who only publish books they genuinely like instead of trying to second-guess the marketplace. Because of this, they often score some real surprise successes. Before submitting your book to the small presses however, do them the courtesy of treating them professionally. Make sure you get hold of some of their other titles. Read them. Follow the publisher's submission guidelines carefully.

If you go with a small press it may be unlikely that you'll be able to stroll into your local Waterstone's or Barnes and Noble and see the book on the shelf. But direct sales from publishers are becoming more important, even for the big companies. And the one big advantage of the rise of Amazon is that there now exists a warehouse where readers can get hold of virtually every book that there has ever been. Books stay on the shelves of bookshops for a shorter time than ever before but, paradoxically, they remain available forever.

Coping with rejection

Who knew that the rejections you need are those of the most crushing kind? Nice ones are just too upsetting.

When my agent started sending out my first book she chose eight editors. The responses could be filed into three sets: the brutally dismissive (2), the lukewarm (2) and the heartbreakingly enthusiastic (4). During that whole painful process I discovered the truth that being turned down by someone who says that they 'absolutely loved' the book is far harder to deal with than the ones who give a curt 'this is not for me'. It's because it seems to leave you with nowhere to go. If even the editors that love the book won't put it out, what do you do then?

You write another book, that's what.

If you're at an earlier stage than this and getting rejections from agents or publishers that keep mentioning the same things (lack of pace, too much back story, etc.) then perhaps you need to rework your manuscript once more, addressing these concerns.

You can always console yourself with the thought that J. K. Rowling's book *Harry Potter and The Philosopher's Stone* was turned down by nine publishers, Stephen King was rejected 84 times before publishing his first short story. Robert Pirsig was turned down by a staggering 122 publishers before going on to sell millions of his classic *Zen and the Art of Motorcycle Maintenance*. Even Zadie Smith was rejected by HarperCollins before all her recent successes with Penguin.

Self-publishing

There exist a number of companies who will agree, for a fee, to publish your book. This is known as vanity publishing and something to be avoided unless you are (a) very wealthy and (b) very self-confident.

You can, of course, become a publisher yourself and control the whole process from editing and cover design, to marketing and distribution. I would avoid this too, except as a last resort.

Part of the desire to be published springs from the need for validation. We need to know if what we have to say is worth hearing. And how can we know that if we have become our own publisher? It is important for your self-esteem as a writer to know that others have invested *their* precious time, talent and energy into your work. Self-publishing feels a little like buying friends to me. Slightly demeaning. And what are you going to do with all those books once they are back from the printers?

My only qualification to this would be if you are exceptionally elderly or exceptionally ill and want to leave your writings in a presentable form for your family. When you genuinely just don't have the time to wait for publishers to discover you.

Ready to go?

1 Write for ten minutes. Yes, right now.
2 Find a regular time in your daily schedule when you can write.
3 Join a writers' group.
4 Look up the Arvon Foundation website (or order the brochure).
5 Tell everyone you know that you are a writer. Get them to take you seriously.
6 Explore writing courses at your local college or university.
7 Make contact with your nearest Arts Centre and find out about live literature events.
8 Compare your most recent piece of writing with the very first things you wrote.
9 Congratulate yourself on your progress. Have some cake, a biscuit or a beer. Buy yourself something.
10 Read a book.

I've said it before, I'll say it again: make sure you always have a notebook.

Notes

Notes